IMAGES
of America

NATICK

The Natick Historical Society and Museum was established in 1870 as the Historical, Natural History & Library Society of South Natick to preserve the history of the town. Under the will of Oliver Bacon, the Bacon Free Library was built in 1880 to accommodate a free library and to provide a permanent home for the historical society, two separate entities. The library and the historical society museum are located at 58 Eliot Street, close by the South Natick Dam.

IMAGES

of America

NATICK

Anne K. Schaller and Janice A. Prescott
Natick Historical Society

ARCADIA

Published by Arcadia Publishing,
an imprint of Tempus Publishing, Inc.
2 Cumberland Street
Charleston, SC 29401

Printed in Great Britain.

Library of Congress Catalog Card Number: 98-88061

For all general information contact Arcadia Publishing at:
Telephone 843-853-2070
Fax 843-853-0044
E-Mail arcadia@charleston.net

For customer service and orders:
Toll-Free 1-888-313-BOOK

Visit us on the internet at http://www.arcadiaimages.com

Edgar S. Hayes advertised as a landscape photographer, and this interest led him to photograph many views of Natick, amassing a very large glass slide collection. In the 1890s, he published a photo album, entitled *Natick Illustrated*, with many views of the town. Both the Town of Natick and the Natick Historical Society are indebted to him for a large portion of their photo collections. Born in 1845, he died in 1899. (Natick Historical Society Collections.)

CONTENTS

ACKNOWLEDGMENTS

On behalf of the Natick Historical Society, Anne K. Schaller and Jan Prescott would like to share our pleasure in presenting this pictorial history, *Images of Natick*.

Editorial Committee:
    Jan Prescott and Anne K. Schaller, authors and editors
    Paul H. Curtiss Jr., M.D.
    Frederick F. Schaller Jr.

Special Appreciation:
    John F. Sullivan, Esq., sports photos and captions
    Dorothy Deslongchamps, Natick history expert
    Tracy D. Schaller, computer set-up, ads, and releases

Research Committee:
    Jan Prescott
    Anne K. Schaller
    Dorothy Deslongchamps
    John F. Sullivan
    Frederick F. Schaller Jr.

Consulting and assistance:
    Laurie-Evans Daly, Carolyn Maguire, Framingham Historical Society
    Henry Hicks, Pauline Attridge, Needham Historical Society
    Jameson Enterprises
    Kinko's of Natick, photographic reproduction
    Middlesex News Photo Archives
    Ronald Prescott, computer support
    Victoria Prescott, photo retouching
    Elizabeth A. Schaller, computer consultant
    Robert M. Schaller, photography

Our thanks to the townspeople who took a personal interest in submitting their historical photographs and whose names are listed within the book.
    This book is dedicated to the people of Natick, to each generation born and raised here, to those who left and hold strong bonds, and to newcomers who can be proud of a town so rich in history. Our mission is to preserve the history of Natick from its earliest history to the present through artifacts and archives in our museum and reference library. We take pride in the volunteer efforts that make this possible.

INTRODUCTION

Natick had its beginning in 1651 when the Puritan missionary John Eliot settled a group of "Praying Indians" on land granted by the Massachusetts General Court. The Indians called the settlement Natick, meaning "Place of Hills."

From 1651 until his health declined and his death in 1690, Eliot instructed and preached to the Indians. A school was set up, a government established, and the Indians encouraged to convert to Christianity. Eliot learned their language and, with their help, transcribed the Bible into the Algonquian language.

The land was held in common by the Indians. They held their own meetings and elected their officials. In 1719, the Massachusetts General Court appointed 20 men as proprietors to oversee the sale of any Indian land. By 1746, poverty had forced most of the Indians to sell their land, and Natick had become a white town.

The prosperity of the village was destroyed when King Philip, a son of Chief Massasoit, attacked white settlers, causing such fear that, in 1675, the Indians were restricted to their villages. In October of that year, over Eliot's protests, the Natick Indians were moved to Deer Island in Boston Harbor. Many did not survive the cold and lack of food. Those that returned found their homes destroyed.

At Eliot's death in 1690, Takawampbait, an Indian whom Eliot ordained, carried on Eliot's mission until his own death in 1716. Two other Indian preachers, Josiah Shonks and John Nemunin, with assistance from Gookin of Sherborn, filled the Indian pulpit until the New England Company sent, first, Rev. Oliver Peabody and, later, Stephen Badger to serve at the Indian Church.

As white settlers moved in, Natick developed as three distinct villages, each on a stage route. In each village there was a tavern; Felchville Tavern was in the north, Morse Tavern in the center, and the Morrill Tavern in the south. These taverns served as inns and meeting places.

In this period, the "Meetinghouse Dispute" erupted. The people in the northern part of the town wanted a church nearer to the center of town rather than support the Indian Church in the southern section. This dispute continued over a period of more than 60 years.

On April 19, 1775, Natick sent 18 minutemen under the leadership of Capt. David Morse to repel the British. During the Revolutionary War period, 174 men out of a population of 534 were to see service in the Continental Army. In 1778, Natick voted to reject the Constitution, but Natick's leaders pledged to support the new government.

After the war, attention returned to the meetinghouse dispute. The church could not relocate without court approval. The people in the southern section petitioned to become a separate town but were denied. The court resolved this issue in 1797 by restoring the "Needham Leg" to Natick. By this time, the Indian Church had dissolved; the congregation dispersed to other parishes. The church building fell in disrepair. It was not until 1828 that a new church was built, the South Parish, now incorporated as the Eliot Church. It is the fifth church on the site.

The original location of the Indian Plantation along the Charles River was probably chosen because the shallow rapids made the fishing easier, especially with the spring spawning runs. The rapids also made possible the building of water-powered mills, first the gristmill and sawmills, later nail making and woodturning, especially for the wheelwright.

In the 18th century, the villages were almost self-sustaining agrarian communities, able to satisfy most of their needs. The shoe industry started as a cottage industry but, by the beginning of the 19th century, began to be concentrated in factories where there was specialized machinery. Piecework in the homes was still an important part of the process. Work was given out and picked up regularly by runners.

In 1836, the Boston and Albany Railroad came through Natick Center. The town growth was to be concentrated here. By 1880, there were 23 shoe factories in the town. The brogan, a work shoe, was the main product. There was also the Harwood and Sons baseball factory, the first baseball maker in the country, and it was here where the figure-eight stitched cover was developed. Natick was a bustling town. There were shirt factories, wagon and carriage makers, to name a few manufacturers, as well as a number of large greenhouses.

Two disastrous fires occurred; one was in 1872 in South Natick, the other in 1874 in Natick Center. Businesses were quickly rebuilt larger than before. Saturday night, as people did their shopping, was the busiest time of the week. This custom persisted as long as the six-day work week prevailed. The Great Depression of the 20th century saw the close of many businesses, and the shoe business migrated elsewhere.

In the Depression years, Worcester Road was rebuilt as a divided highway with four lanes. After the end of World War II, shopping malls lured customers away from the local merchants. Natick became predominately a residential town. What remained were primarily the service functions: banks, post office, municipal services, medical and hospital facilities, and a range of services from dance instruction to hardware stores.

Natick can boast of a number of historic figures: John Eliot, the Puritan minister; Henry Wilson, "The Natick Cobbler" who later moved into politics and became the Vice-President under Ulysses S. Grant; Harriet Beecher Stowe, "the little woman who started the Civil War" and the author of *Uncle Tom's Cabin* and *Oldtown Folks*; Alexander Wheelock Thayer, consul to Trieste and the author of the definitive biography of Ludwig von Beethoven; Horatio Alger Jr., minister and author of books with the "rags to riches" theme; Henry Bacon, the designer of the Lincoln Memorial in Washington, D.C. and the World War Memorial at Yale University. In keeping with the town slogan, "Home of Champions," the new century will likely see many names added to this list.

In compiling this book we have tried to cover the period from 1651 to 1950 chronologically within the chapters. Restricted in length and design, we could not include all the interesting events and the many people who have added so much to the history of our town.

One
THE EARLY YEARS
1651–1800

This type of wigwam was typical of the Natick area. It consisted of a framework of long poles covered with mats, had a central hearth and smoke-hole, and one or two mat doors. Tradition says that only a few Indians moved to English-style houses because of the difficulty of heating them. (Courtesy William L. Biggart Jr.)

Pleasant St. Bridge over Charles River,
So. Natick, Mass.

The Eliot Bridge is located on Pleasant Street, South Natick. Originally a foot bridge built by the Indians in the autumn of 1651, it was 80 feet long and made of wood on a stone foundation with a 9-foot arch. The bridge was located at a ford or "common passage" of the river, which divided the "Indian planting grounds" and pasturage from their dwellings. (NHS Collections.)

On May 31, 1670, the Indians inhabiting the town of Natick requested that the general court grant them a brand to distinguish their cattle from others. It was ordered that a bow and arrow be the brand mark, possibly the first one to be used in America. It is the trademark of the Natick Historical Society. (NHS Collections.)

10

The "Apostle to the Indians," John Eliot (1604–1690) was born in Widford, England, and educated at Christ College, Cambridge. He immigrated to New England in 1631 and was pastor of the church in Roxbury from 1632 until his death. Eliot began preaching to the Indians at Nonantum in 1646, first in English and later in their own language. He was instrumental in the founding in England of the Society for the Propagation of the Gospel in New England by Parliament. He assisted in the organization of 14 Christian-Indian communities. King Philip's War caused the decline of the "praying villages" after the Indians were sent to Deer Island where they endured such hardships that few returned. Eliot also helped write the *Bay Psalm Book* and was the author of many other books and religious treatises, including the Bible that he translated into the Algonquian dialect. (Courtesy the Huntington Library, Art Collections, and Botanical Gardens, San Marino, California.)

Long houses were large dwellings that sheltered several families or were used when tribesmen gathered together. These dwellings were sometimes palisaded. William Bigelow, in his *History of Natick* (1830), states that the outline of the palisade around the first meetinghouse could be traced when the ground was broken in 1828 for the construction of the "South Parish in Natick," now the Eliot Church. (Courtesy artist Rick Keene.)

John Rogers (1829–1904), a sculptor, was a trained engineer whose failing eyesight turned him to modeling as a pastime. By the end of the Civil War, his "Groups," many with abolitionist themes, were popular. His tribute to Eliot and the Praying Indians was done in more than one version but never cast in bronze. (NHS Collections.)

The Eliot Oak, according to tradition, was located on the spot just east of the Eliot Church in South Natick where Eliot preached to the Indians in 1651. When the gas pipes were laid on Eliot Street, the roots were damaged and the tree died. It was removed in 1936. The site is marked with a stone and a plaque. (NHS Collections.)

The Eliot Plaque in the triangle of Union and Eliot Streets near where the Eliot Oak once stood reads, "In Reverent Memory of John Eliot—Born in England—Died in Roxbury—Lover of God —Lover of Men—Seeker of the Christian Commonwealth—Who on this spot preached to his friends the Indians in their own tongue the mercies and the laws of The Eternal." (NHS Collections.)

A mural of John Eliot and the Praying Indians is located in the old Hall of Flags in the Massachusetts State House. This was painted by Henry Oliver Walker (1843–1929) in 1903. (NHS Collections.)

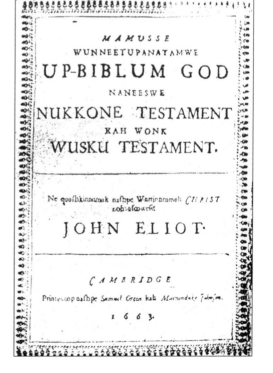

This is the title page of the Eliot Bible in the Algonquian dialect printed by Samuel Green at Cambridge, Massachusetts, with the help of the Indian, "James Rumneymarsh," called the "Printer." In 1663, the complete Bible was printed in an edition of 2,000 copies. Many Bibles were destroyed in King Philip's War and a second edition was printed to replace those lost. (NHS Collections.)

The Indian Burying Ground on Pond Street in Natick Center was part of the 100 acres set apart by the Indians in 1719 for the support of the minister. This was called the Ministerial Lot. The ground was first opened in 1745. The Wamsquon Association, formed in 1800, erected a suitable monument and maintained the grounds. The land was deeded to the town by the Congregational church in the 1970s. (NHS Collections.)

The Eliot Monument was erected on the grounds of the Bacon Free Library in South Natick in October 1847 through the efforts of Rev. Thomas B. Gannett, Henry Wilson, and others. The monument reads, "Erected to the memory of John Eliot, the Apostle to the Indians, as well as, to the memory of the natives who sleep here in its immediate vicinity." (Courtesy Lawrence J. Branagan.)

15

The Indian Burying Ground in South Natick is partially located on the grounds of the Bacon Free Library. Originally, it covered a large area in and around the square. The location is known because of the disturbance of several graves during the construction of the 1828 Eliot Church, the Bacon Free Library, the laying of water pipes, and road work in the square. From the stone marker on the library grounds, the line went east 450 feet to the site of the Eliot Oak by the fire station, then west to a point in the old schoolyard, now Natick Commons, an office building, then south on the west side of Eliot Street for 400 feet, crossing Eliot Street 100 feet to the southwest corner of the Bacon Free Library grounds and east to the monument. Indian graves were unmarked except for Daniel Takawampbait, so the location of individual graves is unknown. (NHS Collections.)

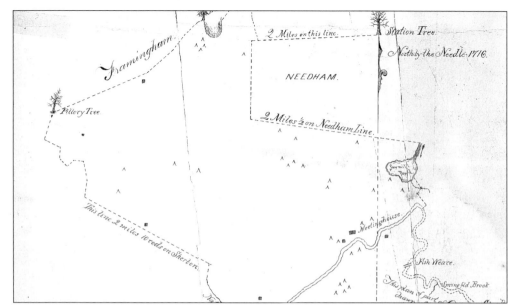

This map is a plan of Natick Township containing 8,062 acres of the "River and Ponds comprehended." It was laid down by a scale of 200 rods to the inch and is signed by John Jones, surveyor, in 1745. The notation of 1716 "by the needle" is a compass date. The station tree at the upper right-hand bound of the map still stands on Winter Street. (NHS Collections.)

The station tree (1749), located on Winter Street, is a famous landmark used by the earliest surveyors. It now marks the boundary line between Natick and Weston. The tree is a black oak and estimated to be over 500 years old. In the early years, it marked the northeast corner of the Needham Leg. (NHS Collections.)

The Lake Cochituate Culvert is a stone bridge used by the Indians as an ancient "crossing" or fording place and as a fishing area. It connects the second and third bodies of Lake Cochituate. Today, Boston Scientific skirts the shore. The Indians would travel along the shores and cross to the path now called Speen Street in order to travel south. (NHS Collections.)

PHILIP. *KING* of Mount Hope.

King Philip was the son of Massasoit, the chief of the Wampanoag Tribe who befriended the Pilgrims. After the death of Massasoit, his eldest son, Alexander, became chief and tried to restore the tribe's lands and rights. After Alexander's death, Philip followed in his footsteps. He gathered tribes from Long Island Sound and as far north as Maine for the bloody conflict called King Philip's War. (Courtesy American Antiquarian Society.)

At the beginning of King Philip's War in 1675, the Natick Indians were sent to Deer Island in outer Boston Harbor where many died of starvation and exposure. This mural of Eliot and the departure of the Indians is located at the Natick Post Office on Common Street. It was painted in 1937 by artist Hollis Holbrook of Natick, a graduate of Yale University and the Massachusetts College of Art. (NHS Collections.)

The Daniel Takawambpait memorial can be found today on the east lawn of the Eliot Church, and his footstone is located in the northwest wall of the Bacon Free Library. This marker stood for many years at the edge of the property at 2 Pleasant Street, South Natick. (Courtesy Lawrence J. Branagan.)

The Takawambpait Pulpit Desk is said to have been built by two members of the Indian congregation at South Natick between 1676 and 1678. Carved on all sides, the desk has deer feet. A slant top and small drawer complete the design of this original piece. The desk was the possession of Daniel Takawambpait until his death in 1716. (NHS Collections.)

Rev. Oliver Peabody accepted the invitation from the Board of Commissioners for the Propagation of the Gospel in New England to become the minister to revive the work of Eliot's Indian mission. He preached for the first time on August 6, 1721, when there were but two white families in the town. Peabody preached for 31 years. He died in 1752. (NHS Collections.)

Stephen Badger, born in Charlestown, Massachusetts, was educated at Harvard, graduating in 1747 with two degrees. He came to the Indian Church at South Natick in 1753, following the death of Oliver Peabody. He was the second white minister to follow Eliot, and he preached for 45 years. His first wife was Abigail Hill, with whom he had six children. After Abigail's death, he married Sarah Griffin Gould of Boston. (Courtesy of Frederic Detwiller.)

The house at 87 Eliot Street was built in 1753 for Stephen Badger. On the ceiling of the minister's study were marks of the sounding board from the earlier church. At the street, a stone marker in the wall stands where a friendship elm was planted by the Indians to honor Badger. The house was restored to its original condition in the 1950s by Ruth and Walterpeinze. (NHS Collections.)

The first meetinghouse at Natick Center was built in 1799 on the site of the present Congregational church. In 1802, known as the First Congregational Church, the meetinghouse began with 23 members, some of whom had been members of the Indian Church. This wooden church was replaced with a brick edifice and the wooden building moved across the street next to the Clark Block. (NHS Collections.)

Patience Pease, one of the last known full-blooded Natick Indians, was born in 1829. She married Amos Augustine Blodgett, a white man, and together they had four children. She was the granddaughter of Hannah Dexter, a famous Indian doctor who lived on the Indian Farm on Glen Street. Pease is buried in Glenwood Cemetery with her people. (NHS Collections.)

Two

EARLY SETTLERS, FARMS, AND MILLS

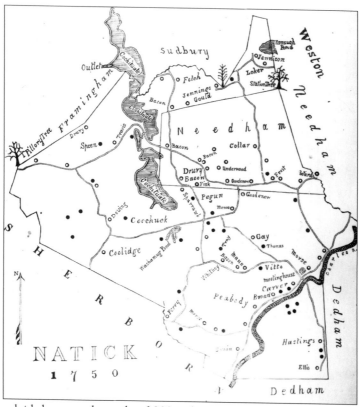

The 1749 map laid down to the scale of 200 rods to an inch in 1749 by Samuel Livermore, surveyor, is a plan of the Natick Parish. The open circles are English houses, and the black circles are Indian houses and wigwams. The eastern boundary of the town was changed in 1797 when Natick was given the wedge-shaped tract of land labeled Needham, generally referred to as the Needham Leg. (NHS Collections.)

This house on South Street was built by the early settler Thomas Sawin, who came from Sherborn before 1718 to build a gristmill at the request of the Indians. The first mill was on the Charles River well above the present dam. A second mill was subsequently built farther up the river. The third dam was on Indian Brook, near the house. During the Revolution, Sawin's was a warning house. (NHS Collections.)

The Farris house was built on Walnut Street in 1761. William Farris served as a captain in Governor William Shirley's regiment in 1745 before moving to Natick from Cambridge. In Natick, he was a justice of the peace. During the Revolution, oxen from Farris Farm helped haul cannon from Fort Ticonderoga to Boston. (NHS Collections.)

The Robert Jennison House was built in the early 1700s. Before its renovation in 1926, the farmhouse had no light, heat, or water, and the fireplace room had a packed dirt floor. Jennison was one of Natick's first selectmen, soldiers, house wrights, and fence viewers. (NHS Collections.)

The Sidney Colburn family farm was located on Worcester Road on the westbound side east of the Route 9-27 Shopping Center. (NHS Collections.)

The Felch-Hammond house is located on the bend of North Main Street near the Cochituate town line. A very old house, it was said to have been owned by Ebenezer Felch, the first Felch in Natick. Later, the Hammond family lived there for many years. Two feuding brothers painted each side of the house a different color. From the front, it looks as though two houses of different periods had been welded together. (NHS Collections.)

The Stephen Bacon house on North Main Street was built in 1704 and is a typical farmhouse of the period. One of the six farms in the Needham Leg in 1724, it was a warning center during the Revolution for the north section of town. Lt. John Bacon, born in this house, died in the Battle of Lexington on April 19, 1775. The first public school classes were held here. (NHS Collections.)

Henry F. Felch lived on the corner of Park Avenue and Bacon Street in the area known as Felchville, where he raised prize chickens. (NHS Collections.)

Isaac K. Felch became a breeder of thoroughbred poultry and an author of books on the subject. Isaac, a member of one of the important families of shoe manufacturers, became interested in poultry at a very young age. He eventually became a traveling agent selling shoes out west, but he ended up selling more chickens than shoes by showing pictures of his prize stock. In the west, he was nicknamed the "Chicken Traveler." (NHS Collections.)

The Perry Farm was located just west of the Henry Wilson Shoe Shop in West Natick. In 1834, William Perry started his shoe business in West Natick. Two years later, he moved it to South Natick and later to Center Street. Perry introduced the first leather splitting and skiving machine in Natick. William was one of eight brothers, all of whom were involved in shoe manufacturing. (NHS Collections.)

This house at 31 Hartford Street is on land once owned by the Speen family of Indians. It included 100 acres on this old road to Connecticut. The recorded history of the house begins with the Travis family, c. 1733. In 1814, during the reconstruction of the house, young Daniel Travis and Henry Coggin were both killed by falling timbers. (NHS Collections.)

Here is the Winona Farm milk delivery wagon. Originally, Winona Farm was solely a dairy farm, with about 50 head of cattle, operated by Mrs. Ernest Burks. Located on Union Street, it no longer operates as a dairy, but animals are still kept there. (NHS Collections.)

The original Luther Broad house at 98 Union Street is said to have been built by John Gay around 1714 and rebuilt after it was sold to Thomas Broad. The Shoe Factory on the left was made into a home by Josephine and Richard Favour. There was a working orchard and, behind the barn, was the pasture. (Courtesy Favour H. Slater.)

The Langdon Moore farm of 120 acres covered most of Pine Street and once extended to the west bound side of Route 9. Langdon W. Moore was the principal conspirator in robbing the Concord Bank of over $300,000 in bonds and cash. Lyman C. Brown, a later owner of the farm, sold spring water and eggs. His son Lyman A. Brown, kept the farm and had a large dairy business. (NHS Collections.)

Aaron Greenwood and Sally Kimball Greenwood are seen here walking down a country lane wearing their wedding hats. These hats are on display at the Natick Historical Society Museum. (NHS Collections.)

The Bacon Farm at 185 Eliot Street has overlooked the Charles River for 230 years. The Bacons purchased land from Rev. Oliver Peabody and land across the river from the Indians. A beam inscribed "1770, Sep. 10" records when minuteman Oliver Bacon rebuilt the old saltbox. Oliver's son, "Pump" John, was the grandfather of the Oliver Bacon who gave the town the Bacon Free Library in memory of his wife, Sarah Griffin Bigelow. (NHS Collections.)

Today called Carver Hill Farm, the Bacon place on Eliot Street has had several names. Remodeled by the Rudds in the 1890s, it was called Orrocco Farm. The farm buildings were greatly expanded to include space for 150 cows and 12 horses, and the house was enlarged and remodeled. Owned by the Barrs in the 1920s, the Greggs restored it in 1934. The Taylor family made it their home for 50 years. (Courtesy Frederic Detwiller.)

Lookout Farm is located on Pleasant Street in South Natick. Purchased from the Indians by David Morse and occupied by Morse heirs for three-quarters of a century, it was known as Morse Farm. Purchased by Elijah Perry in 1816, it was sold again in 1856 to William T. Hanchett. It later came into the possession of the Whittemore Brothers who gave it its present name. (Courtesy Marcia Tompkins Saunders.)

The first Thomas Sawin was given land and water rights by the Indians so that he could build a gristmill with the only stipulation being that their corn be ground first. In 1720, the dam and gristmill was built across the Charles River near Hezekiah Broad's. Three years later, it was removed to Indian Brook. In 1858, John Andrew Morse bought the mill lot with its buildings and water rights and called it Morse's Mills. (NHS Collections.)

Preston C. Morse was a mechanical genius who invented and produced many devices in his machine shop in the old Morse Gristmill. Among them were temperature controls for incubators, an improved cranberry harvester, dynamos, and motors. A telephone line and an electric clock, both of his own manufacture, worked between his house and shop. He made metal castings of small parts for his various inventions. (NHS Collections.)

After John Andrew Morse died, the sawmill was no longer used. His son, Preston Morse, kept the workshop and repaired automobiles. The sawmill burned in 1918, and, before his death in 1929, Preston sold all the mill property to Carl S. Stillman. The Stillman family gave the property to the Massachusetts Audubon Society in 1968. It is now a part of the Broadmoor Wildlife Sanctuary. (NHS Collections.)

The site of the first Sawin dam and mill became the property of Hezekiah Broad, which, in 1755, he sold to Matthew Hastings. The people of Medfield complained of persistent flooding so the mill was moved to the present dam site. In 1815, Deacon William Bigelow purchased and rebuilt the mills located directly behind the Bacon Free Library. Now, the grindstones can be seen in the Old Town Park. (NHS Collections.)

The icehouse of the Dover Ice Company was built on Eliot Street in 1885 by Curtis Broad. This building was about a quarter of a mile above the dam, close to the Broad House and across from the Badger place. Broad also had his canoe livery nearby. The icehouse was later sold to William Diehl and burned down in the 1900s. (NHS Collections.)

Curtis Broad was born in 1850 and was a descendant of Major Hezekiah Broad, a soldier in the Revolutionary War. The Broads bought land from the Indians in the early 1700s, and, in 1885, Curtis bought land on Eliot Street. His home was at 94 Eliot Street, and, near it, he had his Dover Ice Company and his boat and canoe livery. (NHS Collections.)

When John Hill settled in Natick in 1899 and assumed ownership of the icehouse, the company boasted three wagons. The icehouse was on Pond Street, west of and adjacent to the former water pumping station on Dug Pond. Ice was cut for the first time in the winter of 1900 and for the last in 1930–31. When refrigeration was introduced, a plant was erected on West Central Street. (NHS Collections.)

Hill's Icehouse was on Dug Pond. Six inches of ice was needed to support two horses. Ice was marked in 22-inch widths by a horse-drawn saw. Blocks 22 by 44 inches were moved up a conveyor for storage in the icehouse. The company supplied ten surrounding towns. The old foundation is now used by the high school classes for graffiti. (Courtesy John A. Hill Jr.)

The Williamson Cider Mill, one of the oldest and best known, is located at the Everett Street end of Rockland Street. The wooden, three-story building is now owned and operated by Scott Williamson. Its original operation had an old steam-operated screw-type press. The steam power was supplanted by electricity in 1918. (NHS Collections.)

Three
TAVERNS, INNS, AND HOTELS

The 1750s milestone can be seen today in the stone wall in front of 157B Hartford Street. Nathan Stone, an early settler, owned much of the land here where the milestone stands. It alerted stagecoaches that it was 18 more miles to Boston from this point. Hartford Street was an old path and a main thoroughfare to Connecticut. (NHS Collections.)

Peletiah's Tavern at 33–35 Eliot Street was built in 1748 by Peletiah Morse. On a route to New York, the tavern provided rooms to travelers, space for meetings, and boarding for prisoners before other facilities were available. The tavern offered a respite from the cold unheated meetinghouse, and strong drink was commonly served. It was a meeting place for local patriots and served as a town tavern during the Revolutionary War. (NHS Collections.)

Lt. Abel Perry Sr. had a tavern here in 1754. During the Revolutionary period, town meetings were often held here. Perry was an ardent patriot and the owner of a large portion of the present village lying south of Pond Street between Western Avenue and Woodland Street. Located on South Main Street, the tavern was later the home of William Coolidge. (NHS Collections.)

Eliakiam Morrill bought land from Jonathan Carver in 1782. He kept the tavern on Eliot Street for 17 years and was succeeded by several innkeepers. The tavern was destroyed by the South Natick fire of 1872. Goin Bailey built Bailey's Hotel on the Eliot Street site, and his holdings included the schoolhouse building and yard that is now an office building at 49 Eliot Street. (NHS Collections.)

After the Morrill Tavern burned in 1872, Goin Bailey, then proprietor, erected the Bailey Hotel on the site of the old tavern in the summer of 1872. It was the scene of many balls, dinners, parties, and meetings. During this time, large peddlers' wagons came from the city, carrying dry goods, cigars, and other commodities. Bailey also ran an express between South Natick and Wellesley. (NHS Collections.)

Bailey's Hotel was sold to Mrs. R.G. Shaw of Wellesley. Mrs. Shaw renovated it and renamed it the Old Natick Inn. It advertised itself as a "newly re-modeled inn with open fire and suites with bath. Excellent table, afternoon tea, canoes to rent, as well as carriages, sleighs and automobiles. Skating and coasting in winter." The Inn did not prove profitable and was torn down and the land made into the present-day Shaw Park. (NHS Collections.)

The Farris store and post office stood at the foot of Walnut Street at the Worcester Turnpike. Built by William Farris, the store offered refreshments and supplies. Farris became the second postmaster in 1818, a position he held for over 20 years. It is said that when Farris was in the fields he often carried the mail in his hat. The post office was later moved to the center of town. (Courtesy Ellen G. Harwood.)

The Rufus Morse Tavern was located on Central Turnpike (East Central) and Hayes Streets. The first floor was used as family living quarters and a grocery store and the upstairs was used for dances, balls on certain nights, and lectures. In 1845, the Takawampbait Lodge of Odd Fellows meetings were held here. No longer profitable after the railroad was built, it was cut into three parts and moved to different places. (NHS Collections.)

The Felch Tavern, owned by the Felch family, was run by the bachelor Haynes brothers on the northeast corner of Bacon and North Main Streets. Felchville was the village center, and Bacon Street was the main road before the turnpike was built. The brothers were of Indian and African descent on their mother's side, the Ferrits. Competition caused the tavern to close. (NHS Collections.)

At the Cochituate house in the mid- to late 1800s, a person could board by day or week, and particular attention was paid to commercial travelers. The premises were kept first-class at all times and could accommodate some 30 to 40 guests. Food was abundant in quantity and was cooked and served home style. This establishment was located on South Main Street in the Edward Walcott Block. (NHS Collections.)

The Wilson House erected on Summer Street in the 1870s by John Elliot Fiske was a modern building, steam heated and supplied with electric lights. There were stores on the first floor. Opened as a Prohibition hotel, when Fiske sold the property the policy of the hotel was changed. In 1927, two Boston men were operating a still that exploded and destroyed the building. Ironically, the building was across from the police station. (NHS Collections.)

The Hotel Belmont was located at One Summer Street near Washington Street. Its proprietor J.A. Quesnal advertised it in 1904 as the modern hotel in the town. (NHS Collections.)

The Colonial Inn, Natick, Mass.

The Old Colonial Inn on East Central and Clarendon Streets is pictured here. In 1884, this house was occupied by Leander French who had an appliance store in the Eagle Block on Main Street. Considered for use as town hall offices in the 1970s, it has been occupied by various businesses including the *Natick Sun*, which merged with the *Natick Bulletin* in 1989. The structure was removed when the library expanded. (NHS Collections.)

The Sunnyside Hotel building had many names, proprietors, and businesses. It served as a tavern, the first post office, a stagecoach stop, an inn, and a hotel where balls were held. Later, it was used by a carriage factory and the Rex Beverage Company. When Worcester Road was rebuilt around 1931, it is said that the building was relocated to the ramp where a paint store stands today and later torn down. (Courtesy Richard Potter.)

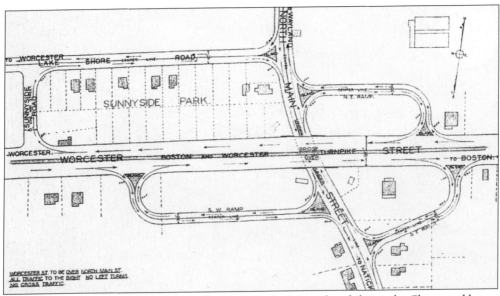

This establishment on Route 9 was called the Elm Park Hotel and, later, the Sherman House. Mr. Sherman built a half-mile race track which included the area along Worcester Road backing up to Lake Shore Road. The race track was known at different times as Elm Park and Sunnyside Park. It was used for sporting events of all kinds including trotting matches, baseball, sprinting, boxing, fairs, and shows. (NHS Collections.)

Four
SHOE MANUFACTURING AND TRANSPORTATION

The Henry Wilson Shoe Shop is located on the corner of West Central and Mill Streets. The structure is an example of a ten-footer. Many homes had these small shops or ells where piecework on shoes was done. Runners delivered the pieces and picked up the finished work. This continued into the 1900s despite the concentration of shoemaking in the large factories of the late 1800s. (NHS Collections.)

This is an example of the type of Brogan first made in Natick. Early shoes were very simple in design and were often without a left or a right and were gradually shaped to the foot with wear. (NHS Collections.)

John B. Walcott, a local shoe manufacturer, built this factory on the corner of Summer and Main Streets that was destroyed in the fire of 1874. He replaced the factory with the new Walcott Building in 1888. Today, it is owned and occupied by the Debsan Company. (NHS Collections.)

Isaac Felch, a carter, is pictured here with a load of leather hides. His teams of horses transported hides, shoes, and other goods between Natick and Boston and as far away as Lake Champlain. He gave up his express business when the railroad was introduced in 1836. (NHS Collections.)

This is a sample of the Pfeiffer Heavy Men's shoe. This is the type of work shoe made right up until the factory closed in the 1930s during the Depression. These shoes were made with rivets for strengthening the stitching and eyelets for laces. Pfeiffer's was the last operating shoe factory in South Natick. (NHS Collections.)

The Pfeiffer shoe factory was located on Water Street in South Natick. William F. Pfeiffer, who learned the shoe trade in Germany, came to Natick in 1853. His first employer was Mr. Cohn, who met immigrants at Castle Island in New York to urge them to come to Natick. Pfeiffer began his own business in 1870 with six employees and, ultimately, employed 200 men making shoes. (NHS Collections.)

Looking at the inside of the Pfeiffer shoe factory, note the line shaft pulleys along the ceiling supplying power to each machine. In the foreground, a man buffs the heel of a finished shoe. On the left are rolling wooden shoe racks used for moving the shoes around the building from one work station to another. The shoes were individually boxed and shipped in large wooden crates. (NHS Collections.)

The Dean Shoe Factory on North Main Street was one of two owned by the Deans. The second was in Cochituate. In Natick, the Dean Shoe Factory employed 2,200 workers and was one of the last shoe factories to operate in Natick. The annex is now occupied by the Whipple Company, makers of Grandmother's Mincemeat. Later, the main building became the Natick Mills, and, today, it has been converted to apartments. (NHS Collections.)

Riley Pebbles came from New Hampshire in 1849, opened a grocery store on South Main Street, and learned to make shoes. In 1853, he began manufacturing and was one of the first men to try labor saving machines. He invented the "beam sole cutting machine," and made a greater variety of shoes than any other Natick manufacturer. He patented the "Pebbles Seamless Balmoral." The Pebbles shoe factory was located at Spring Street near the railroad. (NHS Collections.)

This building on North Avenue was first used by the E.P. Fay Hat manufactory. In 1882, John W. Walcott and Francis Bigelow started the J.W. Walcott Shoe Company. Walcott sold to the Pratt-Reid Shoe Company, and the building was later occupied successively by Brennan Boot and Shoe and Natick Shoe Company. Shoe manufactories moved from location to location as space demands changed. The Duralectra Company is now on the site. (NHS Collections.)

A carriage lines up for a parade on Washington Street. In the background can be seen the Nutt & Pratt Shoe Factory, originally the J.O. Wilson factory erected in the 1860s. One of the largest shoe factories in the state is now the site of the Outdoor Store on North Avenue. Other buildings are the Natick Bowling Alley and the Eaton Harness Company. The Goodnow house, with pillars, is to the far left. (NHS Collections.)

The Winchell Company building, located at Washington Avenue and Cochituate Street, was built before the Civil War for Johnson, Dale & Aldrich. Under successive ownership, five additions were made, the last in 1950 by the Winchell Shoe Company. Winchell specialized in moderately priced men's shoes, the "Faithful Brand," selling from $7.50 to $8.50 a pair. The factory, the last to operate in Natick, closed in 1972 but today houses diverse manufacturing operations. (NHS Collections.)

Walkerville included this train station located on the west side of Speen Street, off West Central Street. A popular social gathering place in the late 1800s, it had a large picnic grove by the lake, a dance hall, a hotel, a mill, and a blacksmith shop. Dr. Joseph Walker built the hotel on Lake Cochituate. He amassed a fortune as a proprietor of "Vinegar Bitters the best bitters there is in town." (NHS Collections.)

The horse car barn stood on East Central Street, east of Union Street. The trolleys traveled to Cochituate via South Avenue and North Main Street. When the line was electrified, a second barn was built on the east side of Union Street, and cars exited onto East Central. The Union Street car barn became the bus barn until service was discontinued in the 1960s. The building then housed businesses before being torn down to make way for apartments. (Courtesy Richard Potter.)

Horse car service was replaced by electric cars around 1895. The Natick and Cochituate line was extended to South Natick and Needham, the Middlesex and Boston line serviced Natick to Newton, and the Worcester Street Railway traveled the Worcester Road. By the early 1900s, it was possible to take a trolley from South Natick to New York City, a three-day trip. People called the yellow cars "Bananas" and the large cars "Battleships." (NHS Collections.)

The Boston and Albany Freight Yard was east of Main Street before the grade change in 1894. The freight house is the nearest building, with Adams Express to the left on South Avenue. The depot in the middle foreground faces South Avenue between Washington and Clarendon Streets. Childs Block at the southwest corner of South Avenue and Washington Street is in the middle background. South Avenue was formerly called Railroad Avenue. (NHS Collections.)

From North Avenue, the pedestrian bridge over the tracks to Washington Street can be seen. The building in the middle is Childs Block, with Washington Hall on the top floor, and Burks, Fiske, and Union Blocks to the right. Behind the Childs Block, the steeple of the Congregational church can be seen in the distance. (NHS Collections.)

This is a view of construction while lowering the train tracks. Leach Block is on the left; on the far right is Natick Beef, with Swift & Company's local distribution plant next door. The house with the pillars is the Goodnow house. The farthest bridge is the Saxonville trestle, and beyond the original Pebbles' Factory. The temporary bridge became the North Main Street Bridge, which is now called the Vietnam Veterans Memorial Bridge. (NHS Collections.)

Pictured is the construction of the lowering of the railroad track. In the background is the J.O. Wilson Shoe factory, later the Nutt and Pratt. Next to that is the Natick Bowling Alley, which had a skating rink at one time, and Eaton Harness. The bowling alley was owned by C.A. Coombs. The area was replaced with houses called Foskett Court, named after the builder, Charles Foskett. (NHS Collections.)

54

The old train depot can be seen here before the tracks were lowered and before the depot was moved farther down the block near Washington Street. Located on South Avenue are Union, Fiske, Burks, and Childs Blocks. The Fiske housed, at different times, Fiske Hardware, Howe Express, Baum Dairy Appliance (makers of the "seal cap"), Burks undertakers, Queenland Robe Company, Perley Snow's second-hand furniture, and Pulsifer & Weatherby Groceries. (NHS Collections.)

In the early 1900s, after the old depot had been moved, the White House Cafe was built. To the right, a ramp leads down to the new station. The area between the ramp and South Avenue is covered with shrubbery. The trolley tracks of the Natick & Cochituate line can be seen coming from North Main Street and continuing down South Avenue. (Courtesy Richard Potter.)

Railroad Station, Natick, Mass.

The new train depot was designed by the firm of Shepley, Rutan and Coolidge, successors to H.H. Richardson. Part of the foundation can still be seen at track level below the commercial block on the north side of South Avenue. (NHS Collections.)

Arriving from the west, the first Boston & Albany train rolls into the new train station in 1895. Spectators crowd the Washington Street Bridge to watch. Pegan Brook that runs beside the tracks has since been put underground. The shoe factory on North Avenue today is the site of the Outdoor Store. (Courtesy Richard Potter.)

Five
BUSINESSES AND TRADES

G.A. Peterson was located on North Avenue in front of the Harwood Baseball Factory. Peterson, one of several such shops in town, specialized in repairing boots and shoes. Work shoes were generally used for hard outdoor work and repairs were often needed. (NHS Collections.)

The Pierce Butler General Blacksmithing Shop was located on the north side of South Avenue. The shoeing of private carriage horses was a specialty. By 1911, automobile work was undertaken, including painting and/or repairing, automobile tops, trims, woodwork, and rubber tires. (NHS Collections.)

The C.M. McKechnie bakery was located at 10 Main Street and specialized in Vienna bread, cake, pastry, and ice cream. They catered weddings and parties as well. In those days, some people were prejudiced against store-bought bread, but McKechnie overcame this and advertised "baked goods and ice cream just as good as the best home-made." (NHS Collections.)

Pictured here is People's Steam Laundry at 7 and 9 Common Street owned by Daniel A. Mahony & Sons, proprietors. In 1886, the laundry was the first establishment of its kind to be opened in Natick. It was equipped to do hotel and family washing. Eventually purchased by the Peoples family, the facility was moved to Middlesex Avenue and managed by Frank Cupples until the business closed. (NHS Collections.)

The Natick Drug Store was located in the space formerly occupied by People's Steam Laundry at 5 Common Street. Next door is E.M. Reed, a second-hand and antique furniture shop. Mr. Reed was born in Rutland, Massachusetts, a descendant of Benjamin Reed, one of the minutemen in the Battle of Lexington. B. Reed was one of the first to lose his life on that memorable field. (NHS Collections.)

The W.E. Daniels Livery, shown in the background, sold horses, supplied boarding, and operated a livery stable. Barges were furnished for picnics and excursions. The livery also supplied hacks for weddings and funerals and maintained a Landau with an experienced driver. The livery was located on Summer Street. Pictured in 1911 are the flowers on Hose No.3 for the funeral of Fireman Frank Pond; the driver is Jack Morris. (NHS Collections.)

Pictured here in the late 1800s is the hearse in front of the John Everett Funeral and Furnishing Undertakers at their first location at 9 East Central Street. (NHS Collections.)

In the late 1800s, the J.B. Whalen Granite and Marble Company was located at 7 East Central Street. The Granite and Marble works later moved to School Street. The police station occupied the area until 1997, and now it is the location of the new Natick Town Hall. John Everett & Sons relocated to 4 Park Street where they are still in business today. (NHS Collections.)

This is a view of West Central Street with its canopy of tall elms. In the Erwin H. Walcott brick block, Cleland, Healy and Underwood had a large store. They sold furniture, wallpaper, curtains, and a variety of small goods. Barnicle and Allen had a grocery here, and, next door, C.W. Perry, Druggist was entrusted with the sale of "spirituous liquors." The Underwood sign can still be seen on the building. (NHS Collections.)

Owned by Arthur W. Palmer, Palmer Clothiers was located in the Clark Block on Main Street. They were in business as long ago as 1880, supplying men's clothing and furnishings. A typical advertisement suggested Palm Beach suits for $12.50 and $15, tropical worsted suits for $25, gabardine suits for $22.50, and ladies suits for $3.50 to $7.50. Palmer Clothiers closed in the 1950s. (NHS Collections.)

Palmer's Men's Clothing Store had imaginative advertising as can be seen by this group of well-dressed gentlemen in a four-in-hand horse-drawn carriage displaying the company banner. (NHS Collections.)

The O.H. Burleigh Insurance Company, General Insurance Agent and Broker, was located in the Odd Fellows Block on the corner of South Main and Pond Streets. The agency, conducted by O.H. Burleigh, was established in 1845 by E.P. Hollis and was one of the best-known enterprises of its kind in the state. (NHS Collections.)

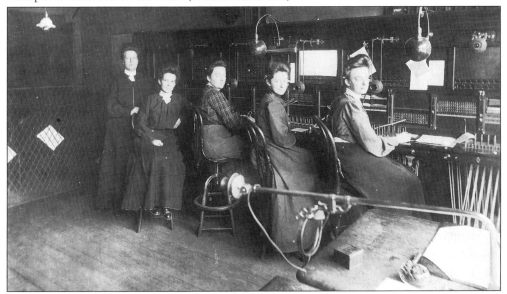

Alice Coveney, a manager, stands at the telephone company switchboard. Before 1910, the New England Telephone and Telegraph Company had space in the Winch Block on South Avenue and was open from 7 a.m. until 8 p.m. In 1937, they moved to new quarters in the Casey Building at the corner of East Central and Washington Streets. Later, they built on East Central Street. (NHS Collections.)

The Burke and Dolan Drug store in the Clark Block on Main Street opened in the late 1890s. Before going into business with Dolan, Walter T. Burke, a native of South Natick, graduated from the Massachusetts College of Pharmacy in 1891. After five years at the pharmacy, he went to Harvard Medical School, graduated in 1900, and set up a medical practice with his brother Michael. (NHS Collections.)

This interior view of the Burke & Dolan Drug store shows the soda fountain and the tobacco display at the front. (NHS Collections.)

Mr. Whitney, pictured here, established a chemical business called Ebenezer Whitney and Company. His largest selling product was "Carbolate of Lime, the Great Disinfectant." A product much in demand in the 19th century, chloride of lime was commonly used to disinfect outhouses. (NHS Collections.)

The W.H. Murphy Company was located in the Eagle Block on Main Street. Murphy sold men's work clothes and furnishings. After the 1874 fire, the Ahern Block was built on this location and is now the site of the Natick Federal Savings Bank. (NHS Collections.)

William D. Parlin employees are seen here in front of the store in Rice Block on the east side of Main Street. The store had three floors. The first floor displayed hardware, agricultural tools, and stoves; the second, doors and metal goods; and the third, window sashes and glazier's room. Parlin's carried most items needed by builders, as well as powder and fertilizers. It was the largest store of its kind in the area. (NHS Collections.)

Originally located in the Eagle Block and then in the Fiske Block on South Avenue, Fiske and Company sold everything from sporting goods to furnaces. Beginning as the firm of Sargent and Heaton, it was succeeded by Heaton & Company, who then sold to Fiske in 1888. Fiske moved into space formerly occupied by the Parlin Company on Main Street. (NHS Collections.)

J.B. Fairbanks, located on Main Street, carried a large assortment of stationery items. They also carried "Fancy Goods" in great variety as can be seen from their advertisement. In later years, they carried mostly office supplies and stationery. (NHS Collections.)

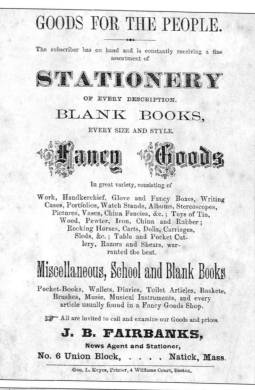

GOODS FOR THE PEOPLE.

The subscriber has on hand and is constantly receiving a fine assortment of

STATIONERY

OF EVERY DESCRIPTION.

BLANK BOOKS,

EVERY SIZE AND STYLE.

Fancy Goods

In great variety, consisting of

Work, Handkerchief, Glove and Fancy Boxes, Writing Cases, Portfolios, Watch Stands, Albums, Stereoscopes, Pictures, Vases, China Fancies, &c.; Toys of Tin, Wood, Pewter, Iron, China and Rubber; Rocking Horses, Carts, Dolls, Carriages, Sleds, &c.; Table and Pocket Cutlery, Razors and Shears, warranted the best.

Miscellaneous, School and Blank Books

Pocket-Books, Wallets, Diaries, Toilet Articles, Baskets, Brushes, Music, Musical Instruments, and every article usually found in a Fancy Goods Shop.

☞ All are invited to call and examine our Goods and prices.

J. B. FAIRBANKS,

News Agent and Stationer,

No. 6 Union Block, ... Natick, Mass.

Geo. L. Keyes, Printer, 4 Williams Court, Boston.

The Natick Beef Company began around 1880 as distributors of Swift's Chicago Dressed Beef. Their local distribution plant was located on North Main Street, just past the new Vietnam Veterans Memorial Bridge. The plant closed in the 1940s, a victim of the wartime meat shortage. The company had served markets, hotels, and restaurants in 15 towns surrounding Natick. (NHS Collections.)

The Brooks Cafe and the Park Cafe diners were the same diner. Mr. Daniels of the Daniels Moving Company owned the horse while Mr. Brooks owned the diner. Later, purchased by the elder Mr. Casey in 1885, Casey would hitch a team of horses to his "lunch cart" and pull it to the Natick Common or around Morse Street, and every evening he would take the diner home. (NHS Collections.)

The Park Cafe, c. 1900, could be seen by the Natick Common with its electrical equipment plugged into a box mounted on a light pole. It was busiest in the evenings and often stayed open until 1 a.m. Pictured here is Wynn Daniels. In 1922, the cafe was sold to Fred Casey who kept it on Kendall Street in Framingham until it was moved to build the Gorman Theater. It was sold to the Stanley Gypsies. (NHS Collections.)

In 1924, proceeds from the sale of the horse-drawn Brook's Cafe were used to purchase Casey's Diner built by the Worcester Lunch Cart Company. In 1926, the yellow and black caboose stood on Washington Street between the Casey home at the corner of East Central and Washington Streets and Carey's Gas Station. The diner was moved to South Avenue in 1977. (Courtesy Fred Casey.)

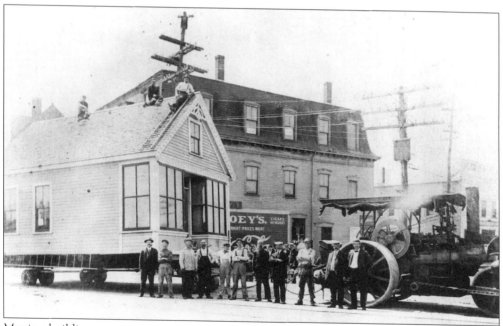

Moving buildings was not uncommon in days gone by. Pictured in the background is Hoey's drugstore in the Ahern Block that burned in the 1900s. (NHS Collections.)

This studio was located on North Avenue. F.J. Williams, or "Williams, the Photographer" as he was more generally known, came from England and founded the enterprise in 1880. He moved to this location in 1887. (NHS Collections.)

Robinson & Jones Company was originally located behind the Leach Block, near the railroad tracks, now the site of the Natick Federal Savings Bank and the Municipal garage. After the tracks were lowered, the business was moved to the freight house yard between Willow and Cochituate Streets. Robinson & Jones dealt in coal, wood, hay, straw, and grain. In 1918, a fire destroyed the buildings and the railroad sheds. (NHS Collections.)

Harrison Harwood moved to Natick and founded the first baseball factory in the world in 1858. Four generations of Harwood men owned and operated the Harwood Baseball Factory. Harrison Harwood Jr., pictured here in 1914 holding the future fourth-generation company president, Richardson Harwood, succeeded his father Harrison Harwood in 1882. Robert W. Harwood, standing, was the third member determined to "Make the Ball that Makes the Game." (Courtesy Ellen G. Harwood.)

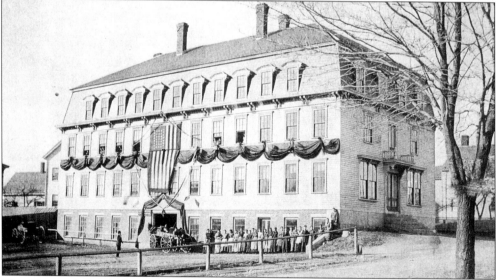

The Harwood Baseball Factory faces North Avenue overlooking Main Street. Harrison Harwood Sr. founded the first baseball factory in 1858 and manufactured the Official League Baseball. The center-wound balls with figure-eight-stitched horsehide covers set the standard for baseballs. Later, cowhide was used to cover softballs. This "cottage industry" included women who stitched balls at home. Wagons delivered piecework and collected the balls for finishing. (Courtesy Ellen G. Harwood.)

The Joe Rock Horse and Carriage House was on West Central Street. Rock was said to have known his horses very well and was considered the best trader in these parts. (NHS Collections.)

In 1899, Harrison L. Whipple, with a recipe from his grandmother, made mincemeat in a 15-gallon iron pot in the back of his grocery store north of the Main Street Bridge. Later, Harrison's son, Lewis E. Whipple, went into commercial production on North Avenue across from the Duralectra Company. In 1945, they moved to 58 North Main Street to the annex of the old Dean Shoe Factory. (NHS Collections.)

Edmund M. Wood was the proprietor of the Waban Conservatories situated on one of the ancient Goodenow farms and part of the Needham Leg. These greenhouses were famous at home and abroad. There were few, if any, rose conservatories in the world to rival them in size. The conservatory was located on Bacon Street on the site of the Jehovah's Witnesses Kingdom Hall. (NHS Collections.)

The Barr Company greenhouses, a South Natick landmark erected in 1898 by John Barr and continued by George Barr, thrived for three generations. The Barrs were known throughout the world for the quality of their prize carnations. When George Barr retired after WW II, his son, John, took over the business in Natick. It was moved to Palm Beach, Florida and later to the west coast where Charles Barr continued the business. (NHS Collections.)

The first electric car in Natick was manufactured by James Belcher in 1905. He named it the Goodnow. Mr. Belcher had a machine shop on North Main Street across from the Natick Beef Company. (NHS Collections.)

The Northway Motors plant was in operation from 1919 to 1923. In those four years, the company manufactured 700 to 800 trucks, and one of those trucks is still privately owned. After the plant closed, it was used as a storage facility by Dennison Manufacturing Company. In 1933, the state purchased the site for a motor transport depot. It was the headquarters of the National Guard on Speen Street near West Central. (NHS Collections.)

Six

BUSINESS BLOCKS AND MAIN STREETS

This is a bird's-eye view of Natick Center in 1887, 13 years after the great fire of 1874. One can see the horse trolley tracks on North Main Street ending at the depot on South Avenue. On the corner of Main Street is the post office (35). On East Central Street is the high school (7), the Methodist church(4), and the Catholic church (5). Other buildings are the J.O. Wilson Shop (10), Pebbles Shop (12), Johnson, Dale, & Aldrich/Winchell Shop (13), and the Clark Block (21). The railroad tracks west of Main Street run along what is now Middlesex Avenue. (NHS Collections.)

This is a view of the west side of Main Street as it looked in 1859. Edward Clark had a grocery store in the wooden building on the corner of Main and West Central Streets. Beyond it are two white clapboard houses, a small park, and the John B. Walcott shoe factory. (NHS Collections.)

West Side North Main St. Natick, 1859.

The west side of Main Street can be seen here as it looked before the fire. The new Clark Block of 1873 is on the left, and the Harwood baseball factory is in the distance. The wooden horse trough in the middle of the intersection of Main and Central Streets was the earliest of its kind in the area. (NHS Collections.)

Here is the old Winch Block on the corner of Main Street and South Avenue as it looked before the fire of 1874. Later, a brick building called Union Block was erected and is now occupied by the U.S. Trust Company. (NHS Collections.)

This shows the east side of Main Street as it looked before the fire of 1874, showing the firehouse and the Woodbury Block. After the fire, the Woodbury Block was rebuilt of brick, three stories high. In 1936, the third floor was removed. Used as a bank building for many years, the third floor has recently been rebuilt by the Middlesex Savings Bank. (NHS Collections.)

Looking south from the railroad tracks one can see the devastation wrought by the fire of 1874. Thirty-seven buildings burned, including the new Clark Block and the Congregational church. The blaze raged for almost four hours, destroying nearly everything on both sides of Main Street from the railroad tracks on the north to the Common on the south and as far east as Washington Street. (NHS Collections.)

This picture was taken by J.W. Woodill in the spring of 1874 from the cupola of the Edward Walcott Block, and it shows the temporary buildings erected by R.E. Farwell, J.B. Fairbanks, W.D. Parlin, and Charles W. Burks. To the far left is the Harwood Baseball Factory and to the far right is the train depot. (NHS Collections.)

Main Street, looking North from The Common, Natick, Mass. 214155

Note the iron water trough that replaced the old wooden one that once stood in the road on Main Street looking north. When the fountain was taken down, an old cistern was uncovered. "Old Mike," as it was called, was moved to the sidewalk at the northwest corner of the Common and became a public drinking fountain. (NHS Collections.)

South Main Street, looking South, Natick, Ma

The Edward Walcott Block and the Odd Fellows Building are located on the corners of Pond Street across from the Common on South Main Street. The cornerstone of the Odd Fellows Building was laid in June 1887. The I.O.O.F. Hall was on the fourth floor, and offices and stores were below. The Takawampbait Lodge, I.O.O.F. was founded in 1845 in the Morse Tavern. (NHS Collections.)

The Edward Walcott, or Middlesex Block, on South Main Street between Pond and West Central Streets was built in 1851 by Edward Walcott. When the high school was first organized in 1852, classes were held on the second floor in Crispin Hall. Many businesses occupied the building, but the best known was the Natick Protective Union, a grocery store. Floors have been removed both by design and by fire. Today, only the first floor remains. (NHS Collections.)

John B. Walcott, a local shoe manufacturer, built the Walcott Building in 1888 on the site of his former factory that was destroyed in the 1874 fire. Today, the building, located on the corner of Main and Summer Streets, is referred to as the Debsan Building. It was the most costly private building built in downtown Natick in the late 1800s with the exception of the Clark Block. (NHS Collections.)

The Ahern Block on Main Street, spared by the fire, was said to have been the old Long Pond Hotel located near the railroad station. It housed various businesses, including J.H. Washburn, the jeweler; the Eaton Company, dealers in dry and fancy goods; a photographer; and a drugstore. (NHS Collections.)

Union Block, located at the corner of Main Street and South Avenue, is shown after the fire of 1874. At this time, it housed the post office and the Howe & Company, Boston Express. The blocks on the east side of Main Street from the corner are Masonic, Rice, and Woodbury. (NHS Collections.)

In this view of South Avenue, the first building looking east beyond the Union Block is the Fiske Block. Built in 1888, Fiske had his second hardware store here before moving to Main Street. The middle building was Burks, and the next was Childs on the corner of South Avenue and Washington Street. Willard Childs was a supplier of thread and glue to the local shoe factories. He had been a gold miner. (NHS Collections.)

The Wood Block, erected by Edward W. Wood, is located on the east side of Washington Street at South Avenue on the corner opposite the Childs Block. A few businesses that occupied the block over the years were Mrs. R.S. Bent's millinery shop, L.A. Perry's bakery, a harness maker, insurance companies, and real estate businesses. (NHS Collections.)

Merchants Block on Eliot Street in South Natick was built by Isaac B. Clark and William Edwards after the fire of 1872. It included a house, Clark's dry goods store, Edwards' clothing store, Cooper's apothecary shop, the post office, and rooms for the historical society. Mrs. Shaw purchased the building, razed it, and built a new one as an annex to the Old Natick Inn. (NHS Collections.)

The fire of 1872 in South Natick started in a dry goods shop. Among the casualties were the premises owned by William Edwards, the Morrill Tavern, the shop of Isaac B. Clark, and the Walker Block. The historical society collections housed in rooms supplied by Mr. Edwards were destroyed. The firehouse was damaged but, later, it was moved farther along the street and restored as a shop. (NHS Collections.)

At the corner of Eliot Street and Mill Lane in South Natick, the Walker building was rebuilt by Eliot Walker after the fire. The post office was here for a short time. In 1886, John Kelly ran a saloon called The Eliot. Fred Hopf purchased the stable behind the building and moved it to Lincoln Street for use as a shoe factory. In 1879, H.H. Hunnewell purchased the Walker land for the Bacon Free Library. (NHS Collections.)

M.V.B. Bartlett built this building at 50 Eliot Street in 1870 and ran a grocery store. Orders could be placed in the morning with the delivery boy and delivered by horse and wagon. In 1910, the business was sold to Joseph Ulrich. Next to the store, Bob Ingalls ran the post office. Eliot Hall, on the top floor, was the scene of many community gatherings. (NHS Collections.)

Shown here is the Martin Van Buren Bartlett Building, *c.* 1910. The Hughes Building to the right at 56 Eliot Street was built in the early 1900s. Frank Pfeiffer had a dry goods store on the ground level, and there was living space on the upper floors. The horse and buggy has begun to share the road with the automobile. (NHS Collections.)

Seen here are the buildings on the north side of Eliot Street as viewed from the west. The building on the left was once the fire station; damaged in the 1872 fire, it was moved to this spot and restored as a shop. Beyond is the annex of the Old Natick Inn, as well as a drugstore, the Inn, and the Eliot Church after it was renovated in 1904. (NHS Collections.)

This scene of South Natick Square shows the Eliot Church, the fifth church on the site of the 1651 Indian meetinghouse. This view was taken before the steeple and windows were changed in 1904. In the foreground is a hydrant and a water pump with tub. In the distance to the far right is the Eliot Oak under which Eliot is said to have preached to the Indians. (NHS Collections.)

This view is looking west towards South Natick Square when the Eliot Oak still stood near the church and the old fire station to the right. The South Natick trolley tracks can be seen coming from Union Street. To the west is the old Bailey's Hotel that is now Shaw Park. (NHS Collections.)

Seven
TOWN DEPARTMENTS AND BENEFACTORS

The first town hall was built in 1841 on the northeast corner of the Common. Moved to the corner of Morse and East Central Streets, it was probably the first official high school. The first library was in the upper story. After 20 years, the building proved too small and was moved to the east side of Washington Street, south of the Wood's Block, and called the Zicko Building. (NHS Collections.)

Oliver Bacon, born in Natick in 1796, was the son of John and Mary Bacon. A farmer, he lived at 87 Eliot Street. His wife, Sarah Bigelow Bacon, established a lending library in her home. After her death, Oliver petitioned the town for permission to build a small library in South Natick as a tribute to his wife. Upon his death, his will provided funds to build the Bacon Free Library. (NHS Collections.)

The Bacon Free Library at 58 Eliot Street, South Natick, was a gift to the people of Natick under the will of Oliver Bacon. Upon his death in 1878, his will provided funds for a library building to replace the small Ladies Social Circle Library and specified that space be provided for the Natick Historical Society. (NHS Collections.)

Leonard Morse was born in 1817 in Sherborn and moved to Natick as a child. He learned the trade of shoemaking and established a factory on South Main Street. His wealth came from investments, real estate, and money lending. Married to Mary Ann Stone, they had no children. Morse's desire to benefit the town was carried out in his wife's will which provided funding for the Leonard Morse Hospital. (Robert Schaller photo of portrait.)

Mary Ann Morse, the widow of Leonard Morse, left her estate to establish and maintain the Leonard Morse Hospital in memory of her husband. The hospital had the capacity to care for about 20 patients. Twenty-seven acres on Union Street provided for additions as needed. The hospital officially opened on March 29, 1899. It was a different Mary Ann Morse who left her estate to the town to build a library. (NHS Collections.)

The Morse Institute is a public library funded by the will of Mary Ann Morse (1825–1862) and accepted by vote at a town meeting. Five trustees were appointed to execute the will, among them were Horatio Alger Sr. and Willard Drury. Through Mr. Drury's efforts, the first decision of its kind in this country took place in the Supreme Judicial Court of the Commonwealth to sustain the establishment of a public library. (NHS Collections.)

The Town Poor Farm was an imposing building on South Main near West Street. The town meeting of 1837 appointed a committee to purchase land for a working farm. In 1849, 108 acres belonging to John W. Perry and Alfred Bacon were acquired. The farm covered what is now Memorial Field, the baseball field, and the town dump. The home was sold in 1936. (NHS Collections.)

In 1896, the West Central Street Sewer pump house was built near Lake Cochituate. The sewage was pumped to sewer beds on the south side of Worcester Road, now the Sherwood Plaza area. The Natick fire department burned the building as a fire exercise in March 1962. The larger timbers burned most of the day. (NHS Collections.)

At one time there was a water pumping station at Dug Pond. The Hill's icehouse, not shown in the picture, was located adjacent to the station. Today, all that can be seen is the foundation of the icehouse where the high school students write their yearly messages. (NHS Collections.)

The Springdale Pumping Station was built in 1917. Willow Bridge, the railroad bridge that crosses Worcester Road (Route 9), can be seen in the background. The pumping station is in use today with new buildings and equipment. (NHS Collections.)

Pictured here is the Mazeppa hand pumper around 1869. In the background is the Civil War Monument and the Edward Walcott Block. (NHS Collections.)

The men of the Union Fire Company stand with their hose and ladder wagon. Fire helmets are mounted above the ladders and the company mascot, a beribboned pet, lies in front. The brass speaking trumpets are filled with flowers for this occasion. The Union Engine House was the old station on the east side of Main Street before the fire of 1874. (NHS Collections.)

This is the Central Fire Station on Summer Street in 1908. At this time, the police station was the small building in the rear. When the fire whistle blew, the horse stalls opened, the horses came out, and the harnesses dropped from the ceiling. The fire whistle could be heard all over town, and, if the horses were working elsewhere and heard the whistle, they would head for the station. (Courtesy Thomas Morris.)

The engine house pictured here was built on the south side of the river on Pleasant Street after the fire of 1872. The basement was used as a lockup and as a place where tramps could be lodged, and the upper story was a tenement. In 1887, it was moved to the lot next to the South Natick Burying Ground on Union Street. (NHS Collections.)

The Fire Department's South Natick steam pumper No. 2 is shown in front of the Old Natick Inn. The spindly wheels show that this was a very early make of fire engine. The driver is Robert Sprowl and riding on the rear is Henry Robbins. (NHS Collections.)

In 1916, the Natick Police Department, from left to right, included: Charles H. Brady, David Church, James Sweeney, Chief Thomas Evans, Edward Murphy, John Topham, William Hogan. The annual budget was $3,000, and the department had 366 arrests that year. Transportation was by horse and buggy, and "hot pursuit" was Chief Tom on a bicycle! In 1874, the town named John Gilson as chief, although many thought paying for a police department was foolish. (NHS Collections.)

The police station and courthouse were opened in 1938 at the corner of East Central and Park Streets. The police occupied the basement and first floor and had an entrance on Park Street. The district court occupied the second floor and had an entrance on East Central Street. Later, the court moved to the former Lincoln School on East Central Street. The new town hall is built on the old police station lot. (Courtesy Lawrence Branagan.)

M. V. M. State Armory,
Natick, Mass.

The Natick State Armory, now used by the National Guard, was dedicated in February 1912 and turned over to Natick's Company "L" of the Massachusetts Volunteer Militia. Forty-six Natick men had seen service in the Spanish-American War in 1898. When built, it was equipped for the use of the militia whose other quarters in town had always been too small. (NHS Collections.)

POST OFFICE, NATICK, MASSACHUSETTS   2333

The post office on Common Street was built in 1936 on the site of the former Wilson Grammar School. The mural of the Indians being taken to Deer Island painted by Hollis Holbrook covers a wall in the foyer. The first post office, established on January 27, 1815, was on the Worcester Turnpike stagecoach line, and Martin Haynes was postmaster. (NHS Collections.)

Eight

SCHOOLS, SPORTS, AND THE "HOME OF CHAMPIONS"

The Wilson Grammar School was built in 1853 on Common Street where the post office stands today. The school was constructed at a cost of $14,000, with funds raised by public subscription. It was a well-built, three-story building of good design with modern heating and an auditorium on the third floor. About 1860, it was used for town gatherings. (NHS Collections.)

The Felch School on North Main Street was built in the 1850s. This building was moved and a new building was erected in 1903. Additions were built in 1907 and 1927. The school was renamed the Nathan B. Goodnow School, but the new name never stuck. In 1932, land deeded by Ellen Murphy was re-covenanted and the Murphy school was built. The Murphy and Felchville schools fell into disrepair and were eventually torn down. (NHS Collections.)

The Walnut Hill School was founded by Miss Bigelow and Miss Conant in 1893. The school buildings were originally part of the estate of Henry Harwood on Walnut and Highland Streets. The beautifully built "noble" stable was converted to classrooms. The second building, called Highland House, was used for dormitories. Today, much enlarged, the school is a thriving performing arts school. (NHS Collections.)

The Natick High School on East Central Street was completed in 1914. The first public function in the auditorium was a gathering of suffragettes to celebrate Natick's First Woman Suffrage Organization. The Class of 1954 was the last to graduate. The building reopened as the Center School for fifth and sixth graders, but was phased out and later remodeled for use as a town hall. (Courtesy of Richard Potter.)

This class, later the Natick High School Class of 1942, was noted for its members who went on to leadership roles in town government. Included are faculty members Misses Finn, Buckley, Hopf, Connolly, Featherstone, and Messrs. Carey and Lane; luminaries Ed Devereaux (town clerk), George Wallace (tree warden), Nick Arthur (assessor), John Moffat (fire captain), Stella Taddeo (administrator), Rita Maloon Grassey (administrator), John Arena (chief of police), and Dick Fahey (fire chief). (Courtesy of Nicholas Arthur.)

The Walnut Hill School golf club, called Highland Golf Links Golf Course, was located behind the Walnut Hill School. This hill was called "Golf Hill." (NHS Collections.)

The Union Ladder Company won the Worlds Hook and Ladder Championship in competition with Westboro, Leominster, and Spencer at Worcester on September 5, 1891, in 58 seconds. The team had to run 220 yards, bring back a ladder wagon, and then hoist a man to a 28-foot platform. In 1892, the company won against Attleboro in 56 seconds. This team inspired the reference to Natick as the "Home of Champions." (NHS Collections.)

Jack Snow, one of the fastest runners in the country in 1905, is shown with starter Jack Hughes. Snow lived with a broken back for five years after being injured in a football game. (NHS Collections.)

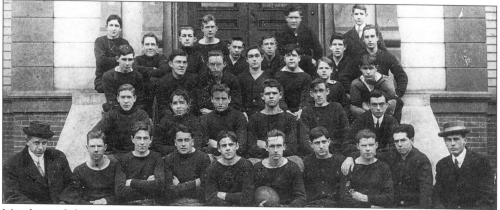

Members of the 1911 football team, from left to right, are as follows: (first row) Dude Pray, Clarence Eldridge, Eddie Casey, Billy Murray, Tom Whalen, Frank Sheehan, Arnold Amoroso, Chick Welch, Vic Doherty, and Squeekie Campbell; (second row) Charlie Sweeney, Scheufle, G. Sellew, Z. O'Rourke, Andy Whalen, and Tricky Murphy; (third row) Punk Mahard, L. Bouret, Doc Grady, Pat Hayden, Dyke Quackenbush, Slip Howard, and C. Brown; (fourth row) Ray McDonald, Francis Murphy, Russell Frye, L. Morse, Tony Sweeney, Maurice McGrath, Ed Kerns, Tom Mallery, H. Meserve, and Jim Mahoney. Murray and Casey went on to Harvard, All-America honors, and a Rose Bowl Championship. (Courtesy of Henry Grady and Bruce Simonds.)

The 1919 girls basketball team, pictured from left to right, are as follows: (front row) Viola McGlone, Esther Yeagher, and Isabelle Brennan; (middle row) Mary Fitzgerald; (back row) Ella Johnson, Lena Pine, and Marion Slamin. Female sports participation in the early 20th century was limited and of a genteel nature. These young women are in basketball attire befitting the time. (Courtesy of Paul Peters, Natick High School athletic director.)

Edward "Ned" Mahan was Harvard football captain in 1915. Mahan is thought to be the greatest all-around athlete of Natick and a major contributor to its reputation as the "Home of Champions." Outstanding in football, baseball, and track, Walter Camp named him fullback on his All-America football team for three consecutive years, 1913–1915. Mahan Field is named for him. (Courtesy of John F. Sullivan, Esq.)

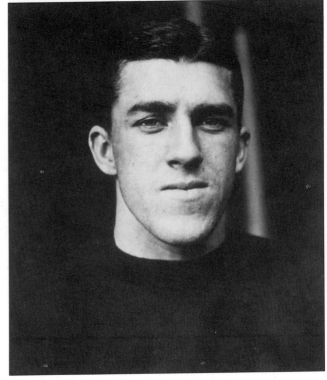

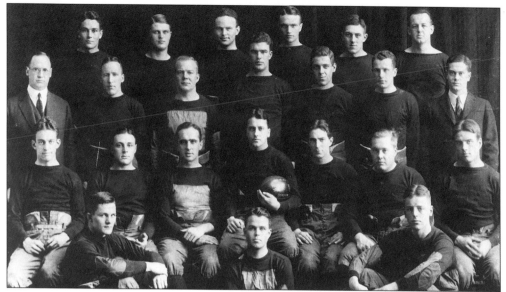

Pictured here is the 1919 Harvard football team, led by Captain Billy Murray and All-America half-back Eddie Casey, both of Natick and heroes of the famed 1911 high school team. Harvard was undefeated and accepted an unexpected invitation to the Rose Bowl game in Pasadena, January 1, 1920. The score was Harvard 7, Oregon 6. Not pictured are Backfield Coach Edward Mahan and Trainer "Pooch" Donovan, both of Natick. (Courtesy of Harvard Archives and John F. Sullivan, Esq.)

The 1925 Natick High basketball varsity, from left to right, are as follows: (front row) Joe Shea, Ted Dumas, Paul Heslin, Fran McGowan, and Joe Byrne; (middle row) Max Mordis, Bill McManus, John Pine, Jerry Morrill, and Yump Wilson; (back row) Packie Garvey, Austin Fitts (manager), Hubba Collins (coach), Ray Tanner (manager), and Jim McGrath. W. Joseph Shea starred as a player at Dean Academy and later served as Natick police chief for many years. (Courtesy of Bruce Simonds and Paul Peters, Natick High School athletic director.)

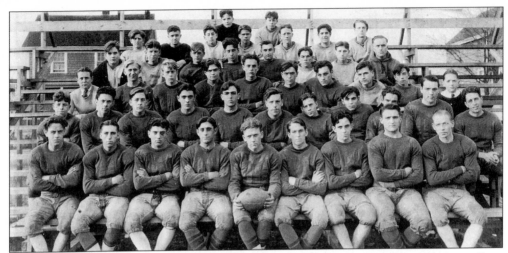

The 1929–1930 football team, from left to right, are as follows; (first row) Jim Chaisson, Foxy
Flumiere, Nicky Christy, George Long, Leo Flynn (captain), Bob Wignot, Bill Morrissey, Pete
Ligori, and Franni Hughes; (second row) Eddie Casey, Bill Hall, Al Johnson, Francis Gagnan,
Phil Woods, Ralph Scholl, George Hall, Salvi Grippi, Eddie Brown, Spit Evans, and Bunny
Green; (third row) Jimmy Carnie, Johnny Hladick, David Mitchell, Russ Hardigan, Dink
Rogers, Dunk McGaughlin, Arthur Taddeo, George Stone, Eddie Mann, and Bobby Gileran;
(fourth row) Fat McRae, Kelly Kline, Grassey, Stevey Rich, Jim Baran, Billy Grady, and Coach
Donahue; (fifth row) Red Pallidino, Joe Estella, Robbins, Lynch, Gallagher, Quatrale, and
Parks; (sixth row) McNichols and Flynn. This team bears familiar Natick names: George Long,
restaurateur; Bill Morrissey, deputy sheriff; Pete Ligori, builder; Art Taddeo, surgeon; Joe
Estella, music teacher; Eddie Casey, school principal; and Mike Quatrale, egg distributor.
(Courtesy of Bruce Simonds.)

Pictured here is a group of
Albanian-American boys,
about 1944, at the corner of
Church and Common
Streets, a neighborhood
then called "Snipe Island."
Clockwise from the top
center are Tom Christie,
Vangie Sticka, Keecho
Sticka, Charlie Christie,
Jim Peters, Charlie Sticka,
and Ted Stamuli.
Representative of Natick's
popular Albanian families,
the Stickas and the
Christies were outstanding
sports figures. Other
sporting family names
included Hladick, Checani,
Ligori, Tutuny, Petro, Argir,
and Zicko. (Courtesy of
James Peters.)

NATICK'S AFTER THE BIG ONE

by Vic Johnson

SCOTT HECKENDORN, RIGHT TACKLE

HEAD COACH JERRY SLAMIN OF NATICK IS DOING OKAY FOR A FIRST-YEAR MAN —8 WINS!

CO-CAPTAIN JOE KANE, QUARTERBACK

BOB GOODALL, L.G.

DICK ROCK, LEFT TACKLE

FRED BRENNEN, CENTER

TED PIERS R.H.B.

L.H.B. JOHN CRISAFULLI

CO-CAPTAIN WALLY MONTGOMERY, RIGHT END

FULLBACK CHARLEY STE IS THE TEAM LEADING SCORE

FRAMINGHAM

BOB COCHRAN, LEFT END

JOE WHITE, RIGHT GUARD

STUDENT MGR. CHARLEY SLAMIN

YOU'LL FIND ASSISTANT COACHES CHARLIE McMANUS AND BOB CARROLL IN THE MIDDLE OF EVERY PRACTICE SESSION

Pictured above is the 1949 Class "C" Champions of Massachusetts. Natick's undefeated and untied record was as follows: Clinton 14–0, Milford 43–9, Wellesley 24–7, Needham 33–14, Marlboro 13–7, Maynard 25–6, Norwood 43–0, Hudson 26–6, and Framingham 39–0. (Courtesy of Paul Peters, Natick High School athletic director.)

The 1950–51 hockey team, Massachusetts State Champions, from left to right, are as follows: (front row) Richard Ciccarelli, John Quilty, George Finley, Charles Tutuny, Thomas Curley, George Morgan, Charles Bassett, Salvi Parrinello, Ronald Flynn, and Peter Stone; (back row) Daniel Whalen, Jon Sheehan, Richard Griffith, Henry Grady, John Carter, Ronald Ellis, William Balcom, Bertold Antelak, William Thomas, Paul Gassett, Donald Griffith, Richard Kane, and Coach Robert Carroll. The team defeated the championship teams of New Hampshire and Rhode Island before falling to St. Domenic's of Maine, a noted hockey powerhouse of New England. (Courtesy of Paul Peters.)

The 1957 basketball team, from left to right, are as follows: (front row) S. Bishop, P. Reynolds, R. Garvey, G. Merten, P. Smith, and J. Tupper; (back row) J. Hassard, J. Stratton, J. Bouzan, T. Kadlik, D. Morgan, B. Carter, W. Barry, R. Canoni, and Coach Francis Carey. Absent from the picture are Clayton Cox and Curt Lund. The team was undefeated in 1957, with 20 consecutive wins and a Class B Championship. This was the first undefeated basketball team in 20 years in the "Home of Champions." (Courtesy of Paul Peters.)

Epilogue

The Hook and Ladder competition required strength and endurance. "Piper" Donovan, the most famous member of the 1891 hook and ladder team that inspired the Natick slogan "Home of Champions," was the first man ever to run 100 yards in 9.6 seconds. The preceding images are only a small part of the illustrious athletic history of Natick. An account of the most recent 35 years must await another time, but a brief mention here of those glory days is imperative. Legendary baseball coach John Carroll won a state record 503 games before 1991, and Natick went to four Super Bowl Championship football games. Star players Darren and Doug Flutie went on to pro careers. Doug was remembered at Boston College for the famous "Hail Mary" pass and the Heisman Trophy. Along the way the Redmen compiled an incredible record of 38 consecutive victories under Coach Tom Lamb, the longest unbeaten streak ever by a Massachusetts Division One high school. (Courtesy of Bob Lesniak.)

Nine

EVENTS, PLACES, AND PEOPLE

The 250th anniversary of the founding of South Natick in 1901 was celebrated with many events. The regatta on the Charles River had canoe races, steam launches, swimming, and water tournaments. In the evening, canoes were decorated with lanterns strung above them. There was a band concert by the Natick Cadet Band, a parade to the schoolhouse hall for a banquet, and addresses by Senator Tirrell and others. Here the crowd is gathered on the shore to watch the regatta. (NHS Collections.)

Located at 50 and 56 Eliot Street, the M.V.B. Bartlett Grocery and the Frank Pfeiffer Boot and Dry Goods Store decorated for the 250th anniversary of Natick in 1901. South Natick was dressed for a celebration on this historical occasion. (NHS Collections.)

The Eliot Church at South Natick Square is decorated in bunting for the celebration of the 250th anniversary of our town. This Eliot Church of 1828 was the fifth church on the site of the Indian meetinghouse and survives today looking very much as it did in 1901. (NHS Collections.)

This photograph shows the east side of Main Street in Natick Center, looking north from the top of the Odd Fellows Building on South Main Street. Downtown was a busy place during the Merchants' Week Celebration of 1908. The horse and buggy still predominated over the motor car. (NHS Collections.)

Natick has always liked a parade. In the 1920s, Mrs. Goldwin P. Holbrook decorated cars for the parade. (NHS Collections.)

The celebration of the 300th anniversary of the town was a week-long spectacular event. Floats and bands made up a large parade. This prize-winning floral float, by DeRosa Florist, carried Miss Natick and her Natickettes. (Courtesy DeRosa Florist.)

During the week-long celebration, many floats were assembled. Here we see a float with an Indian and wigwam reminding the spectators that the town began as an Indian plantation. (Courtesy Middlesex News Archives.)

A large elm stood in front of the house at 95 Eliot Street, the home of Maj. Hezekiah Broad who served under Gen. George Washington during the Revolutionary War. When President Washington was on his way to Boston in 1789 to organize the Continental Army, he is said to have stopped and conferred with Major Broad under this tree. It became known as the "Washington Elm." (NHS Collections.)

The Revolutionary Soldier's Memorial was placed on the library grounds in Natick Center by the Daughters of the American Revolution in 1913 to pay tribute to those Natick men who served to establish our independence. Forty-five of these men are buried in Natick, 13 at North Natick, 15 in the Old Burying Ground in South Natick, 11 in Dell Park, and six in the Boden Lane Cemetery. (NHS Collections.)

Although this advertisement was in the Boston papers, the antislavery movement found strong support in Natick. In 1836, the American Anti-Slavery Society had 163 members in the town. Natick was on a major route along which slaves traveled to Canada. Some individuals who were involved with the Underground Railroad were William Stone at 159 Hartford Street and Edward Walcott on West Central Street. (NHS Collections.)

CAUTION!!

COLORED PEOPLE

OF BOSTON, ONE & ALL,

You are hereby respectfully CAUTIONED and advised, to avoid conversing with the

Watchmen and Police Officers of Boston,

For since the recent ORDER OF THE MAYOR & ALDERMEN, they are empowered to act as

KIDNAPPERS

AND

Slave Catchers,

And they have already been actually employed in KIDNAPPING, CATCHING, AND KEEPING SLAVES. Therefore, if you value your LIBERTY, and the *Welfare of the Fugitives* among you, *Shun* them in every possible manner, as so many *HOUNDS* on the track of the most unfortunate of your race.

Keep a Sharp Look Out for KIDNAPPERS, and have TOP EYE open.

APRIL 24, 1851.

Edward Walcott was born in Danvers and was the eldest of 13. He came to Natick as a child around 1818 where he later purchased land on both sides of West Central Street that extended from Natick Center to the west end of Dell Park Cemetery. A successful businessman, he was active in town affairs. An ardent abolitionist, his home was part of the Underground Railroad. (NHS Collections.)

The Edward Walcott mansion on West Central Street was built in 1853. With 21 rooms and six imported Italian marble fireplaces, the house was given the nickname of "Walcott's Folly." The Walcotts were the town's leading abolitionists. Demolition of the mansion revealed a brick tunnel about 4 feet high that appears to have served as a secret entrance, extending from the cellar to the embankment of the Boston & Albany Railroad. (NHS Collections.)

Born February 16, 1812, Henry Wilson, vice president of the United States under Ulysses S. Grant, was known as "The Natick Cobbler." After his indenture was completed, he walked to Natick from Farmington, New Hampshire. Here he learned shoemaking. The shoe shop located near the corner of West Central and Mill Streets is a memorial to him. His home was at 33 West Central Street. (NHS Collections.)

Henry Wilson died in Washington, D.C., in November 1875 while serving as vice president of the United States. Returned to Natick for burial, he lay in state in Clark's Hall. The funeral was held in the First Congregational Church. A Marine guard accompanied the hearse that was drawn through the streets by four black horses. Wilson is buried with his family in the Old Dell Park Cemetery. Businesses and homes were draped in mourning. (NHS Collections.)

Calvin Stowe was born in Natick in 1802, graduated from Bowdoin College in 1824, and attended Newton Theological Seminary. Married to Harriet Beecher, they had seven children. Harriet Beecher Stowe, an abolitionist, wrote many books, among them *Uncle Tom's Cabin*, which was credited with helping start the Civil War, and *Oldtown Folks*, a fictional novel based on Calvin's family and the people of South Natick. (NHS Collections.)

Built in 1816 by Dr. Alexander Thayer, this house at 2 Pleasant Street, South Natick, is named for its most famous visitor, Harriet Beecher Stowe. Harriet and her husband, Calvin Stowe, stayed here on their lengthy visits to his family in South Natick. Dr. Thayer's son, Alexander Wheelock Thayer, consul to Trieste in the 1890s, was known for his definitive biography of Beethoven. (NHS Collections.)

Civil War veterans are seen here passing in front of the Cochituate House in the Edward Walcott Block on South Main Street at the dedication of the Civil War Monument. (NHS Collections.)

The Civil War Monument on the Common at Natick Center dedicated on July 4, 1867 is inscribed with the names of those who died. At first, the monument stood alone, but, at a later date, four brass cannons on carriages were presented by the government and a wrought-iron fence was placed around the area. (NHS Collections.)

When the Spanish-American War was declared in 1898, Natick men of Company L of the 9th Infantry, Massachusetts Volunteer Militia were called to service and are shown here marching down East Central Street. The town closed down to see the men off to Framingham. The soldiers trained at the Musterfield at the corner of Concord Street and Worcester Road. Later, they moved to Camp Alger in Virginia before seeing action in Cuba. (NHS Collections.)

When WW I was declared, Company L was mobilized and moved to Camp Maguinnesin, Framingham. Over 3,000 residents were on hand to see them off, and the town was decorated with a large flag across Main Street. The first Natick casualty happened in Framingham when Corp. Edward P. Clark was killed by lightning. He was buried with full military honors in Natick. (Courtesy Middlesex News Photo Archives.)

Charles Quincy Tirrell was a Dartmouth graduate, an educator, and a lawyer. In Natick, he served as town moderator and was very active in local and business affairs. In 1881, he was elected to represent this district in the state senate. Subsequently, he was elected to the U.S. Congress where he was interested in education, irrigation in the west, temperance, and was instrumental in the extension of free rural mail delivery. (NHS Collections.)

Horatio Alger, born in Revere, Massachusetts in 1832, was the son of Rev. Horatio Alger Sr. and Olive Fenno. Horatio Jr. was ordained but gave up the ministry for teaching and writing. His most famous books were on the "rags to riches" theme. Most of his life was spent in New York, but he returned to Natick frequently. He died at his sister's home in Natick and is buried in Glenwood Cemetery. (NHS Collections.)

Ten
GOOD TIMES
AND PROSPERITY

The Natick & Cochituate trolley ran from Cochituate via North Main Street, South Avenue, and Union Street to Water Street in South Natick where it crossed the Charles River and continued to Needham. The connection to Needham was added in 1900 but abandoned only a few years later. When there were dances at the Riverside Ballroom, the trolley would wait at the river until the dances were over to take passengers home. (NHS Collections.)

The Riverside Ballroom, owned by the Heinleins, was at the foot of Water Street. On the trolley line, posters advertised the Riverside Ballroom: "Gents 55 cents, Ladies 35 cents." It was a popular gathering place with music, dancing, and prizes. The price was right, and the Heinlein canoe livery was just next door. (NHS Collections.)

Unusual door prizes were the drawing card at the South Natick Ballroom. Sometimes it was a diamond ring, so it paid to hold the lucky number; however, a live pig was an awkward prize to carry home. (NHS Collections.)

The Charles River at South Natick was a popular recreational area for boating, canoeing, and fishing. The trolley bridge carries the canoe livery advertisement: "Canoes stored and to let." Note that cars leave the boathouse every half-hour, and, to the right, the schedule of connections to neighboring towns and to Boston can be seen. (NHS Collections.)

Charles Heinlein, proprietor of the Heinlein Boat and Canoe Livery, advertised his accommodations widely. The Charles River was one of the busiest recreation centers in the town. This canoe livery was destroyed in the hurricane of 1938 and never rebuilt. (NHS Collections.)

Boating on the Charles was enjoyed by many. There were barges, canoes, motorboats, and steamboats. Here we have the Schallers, one of the old South Natick families, steam boating on *Isabel* on the stretch of the river above the Cheney Bridge. It was sometimes necessary to clear the grass from the boat's propeller, and occasional stops for wood were needed. (NHS Collections.)

The workmen, pictured here rebuilding the South Natick Dam in the late 1800s, show the tools of their trades: the shovel, the pick, the broom, the surveyor's rod, and the carpenter with saw. Note the old-fashioned wheelbarrow. (NHS Collections.)

In 1934, the dam at South Natick was rebuilt with concrete and funded by the Emergency Relief Act (ERA). A large crowd gathered for the dedication. Henry Cabot Lodge was one of the speakers from a platform erected in the park. (NHS Collections.)

The canal which crosses Pleasant Street near Glen Street was built in 1838 to furnish water power to the Flax Leather Board Company, who used leather scraps, or "jim pins," to make leather board. The mill was later used by Curtis Paper Company, Eliot Falls Electric Light Company, Boston Bedding Supply Company, Indian Spinning Mills, and Auto Sickle Company. Cross arms on the poles indicate the mill was then supplying electricity to South Natick and Wellesley. (NHS Collections.)

This photo of a Waco plane was taken in the mid-1930s at the airport located behind Wilson Middle School in Wethersfield that was on land now occupied by Fairway Bowling and Natick Office Park. Charlie Paine, one of two WW I pilots with a two-seater, would perform. People stood in line for a dollar a ride, and barnstormers would put on a show for the crowd. (Courtesy John Rossi.)

Saturdays and Sundays were busy days at the airfield with demonstrations and stunt flying. Wethersfield Road, then a runway, was the access to several hangers. The airport was in business only a few years. (Courtesy Mary and Brad Leavitt.)

The Boston Marathon has come through Natick since 1897. In a booklet printed for the 100th anniversary of the marathon celebrated in 1996, it was said that Ellison Brown, a descendant of King Philip, led the marathon twice through Natick on his way to victory in the 1930s. This 1938 photo was taken on East Central Street. (NHS Collections.)

On May 6, 1937, Natickites were eyewitnesses to what was to be the last flight of the German dirigible, Hindenburg, pictured over the Congregational church around noon. Clearly visible was the red, white, and black Nazi swastika emblazoned near the rudders. On landing that evening at Lake Hurst Naval Air Station, New Jersey, the Hindenburg was engulfed in flames. It crashed, killing 37 including one ground crew and severely injuring 62 others. (Courtesy Lawrence J. Branagan.)

NATICK THEATRE

WEEK OF AUG. 15

MONDAY and TUESDAY

TOM MIX

in "The Big Town Roundup"

COMEDY--KINETO

WEDNESDAY and THURSDAY

POLA NEGRI

in "GYPSY BLOOD"

AND

MARY MILES MINTER

in "DON'T CALL ME LITTLE GIRL"

FRIDAY and SATURDAY

SHIRLEY MASON

in "THE LAMP LIGHTER"

COMEDY--NEWS

The Natick Theater on the east side of Washington Street showed silent movies, and later became Kemp's Bowling Alley. Earlier, the Lyric Theater stood at the corner of Washington and Court Streets. The last movie house in downtown Natick was the Colonial Theater on East Central owned by Fred and Nancy Harris. (NHS Collections.)

This is the Natick Drive-In Theater as it looked in 1978. The theater was very popular with young people, and families flocked there with blankets and pillows for the children. The concession stand, with its popcorn and drinks, was a busy place during intermission. Speakers were sandwiched between the windows, and mosquitoes roamed freely among the viewers. The theater stood where the Cloverleaf Mall is today. (Courtesy Ric Getter.)

Camp Pleasant on Lake Cochituate, off Perry Road, was popular, and the shores were lined with tents and summer homes. Camp Tray, near Fiske's Bluff, was built by David Fiske in 1887 on land once owned by the Indian Philip Tray. The trolley on the Cochituate line would stop at "Camp Tray Crossing" on request. In 1848, the city of Boston acquired all rights and water privileges, and public use, except for boating, was prohibited. (NHS Collections.)

Lake Cochituate consists of three lakes in the towns of Wayland, Framingham, and Natick. The Indians called the lake "Cochituate," meaning "place of the rushing torrent," which applied to the lake outlet because of the volume of water in spring. During the 18th century, the Indian name was changed to Long Pond. Later, the old Indian name was restored. Pictured here is the Cochituate Boat Ramp at the State Park. (NHS Collections.)

The Carling Brewery started producing Red Cap Ale and Black Label Beer in 1956 at this Natick location. Said to be the world's most modern brewery at that time, it employed about 250 local residents and became New England's first brewery in more than 40 years. Today, Boston Scientific occupies the building on Worcester Turnpike beside Lake Cochituate. (NHS Collections.)

The U.S. Army Quartermaster Research and Engineering Command, off Kansas Street on Lake Cochituate, came to Natick in the 1950s. It is a laboratory for the armed forces to test and analyze all kinds of material under varying stress and atmospheric conditions. Originally a thousand men and women, 700 of them scientists, were employed here. (NHS Collections.)